THE LAND OF ISRAEL
100 YEARS PLUS 30

THE LAND OF ISRAEL

100 YEARS PLUS 30

A Pictorial Survey by Tim Gidal with Leorah Kroyanker

Steimatzky and Keter Books

Jerusalem

Color Layout by Shlomo Yehudayan
Cover Design: Ziva Sivan

Copyright © by Keter Publishing House, Jerusalem, Ltd., 1978
P.O.B. 7145, Jerusalem, Israel.

Cat. No. 257568
10 9 8 7 6 5 4 3 2 1

ISBN 0–7065 2500 0

Printed by Keterpress Enterprises Ltd., Jerusalem

Printed in Israel

INTRODUCTION

by Julian J. Landau

The first photographs of the Holy Land were taken in 1847, shortly after modern photography was developed. During the 130 years that have elapsed since then, innumerable pictures have captured the landscape of the country, the face of its people, and the configuration of events which have shaped its history and molded its inhabitants.

Photography has accurately and movingly recorded developments in the Land of Israel over the past century and a quarter; the rise and fall of empires which ruled it; the conflicts, both global and local, which racked it; and the dream come-true which reclaimed it.

As a medium, photography is unique. Its ability to recreate the past, to recall what no longer exists and to portray what we have never seen, is unparalleled. It is both a tool and an end, a means to analyze history but also a memory or a glimpse into yesterday.

In both these regards, the century preceding the establishment of the State of Israel, and the 30 years of its existence until today, was a period of much more than passing significance. It was, above all, a time of accomplishment, of life and emotion, of building and reclamation, of goals achieved and surpassed. But it was also a period of turmoil and warfare, of death and destruction, of unresolved conflict and continuing enmity. It was the time of the Zionist dream and the time of its fulfillment.

In the second half of the 19th century, the Holy Land was a neglected and desolate backwater of the declining Ottoman Empire. Despite its emotional and religious significance for Christians, Jews and Moslems the world over, it was not a pleasant place to live in or even to visit. In Jerusalem, for example, some 15,000 inhabitants crowded together in dilapidated houses built around narrow court-yards, seeking refuge within the walls of the city from marauders. The twisting and turning streets were almost always strewn with garbage and often with the carcasses of animals who perished during the frequent droughts. Poverty was the way of life. Travelers and pilgrims, who had weaved their way in small boats through the treacherous rocks at Jaffa port and managed to avoid the fearsome Sheikh at Abu Gosh, as well as other bandits and robbers on the way to Jerusalem, were shocked by the beggars and the filth which greeted them in the Holy City.

Nor was the political situation any more heartening. Rivalry between the various Christian nations for influence and power often led to violence. The Crimean War, for example, broke out in 1853 partially due to the conflict between Russia and France over guardianship of the Holy Places. The Sultan, Abdul Hamid II, tried to preserve the remnants of his power by increasing the number of local officials and strengthening the military forces stationed in the country.

It was, however, during just this period that the country began to awaken. The increased interest which the European powers took in the Holy Land did not bring only clashes. The Palestine Explora-tion Fund, founded in 1865, surveyed the area west of the Jordan River for the first time. That same year telegraphic communications were established in Jerusalem and other important towns. In 1868 the first road suitable for wheeled carriages was completed between Jaffa and Jerusalem, and the country's first railroad, also linking the two cities, was completed in 1892.

But the real seeds of development were sown not by the Christians, but by the Jews. The Damascus Blood Libel of 1840, accusing the Jews of that city of the ritual murder of a Franciscan monk, led, in part, to the advocacy of "normalization" of the Jewish people through settlement in the Holy Land,

5

by such writers as Rabbi Yehuda Alkalai (*Third Redemption*—1843), Rabbi Zvi Kalischer (*Seeking Zion*—1862) and Moses Hess (*Rome and Jerusalem*—1862). Some years later, in 1881, the assassination of Czar Alexander II was followed by a wave of pogroms all over Russia. Many emancipated Russian Jews began, as a result, to advocate a return to the Land of Israel. Inspired by them, and particularly headed by Leon Pinsker, organized groups of the Lovers of Zion and BILU movements made their way to Palestine. The presence of the Zionists was quickly felt in the country. Within a few years new agricultural settlements had been established in the Galilee and in Judea and Samaria. Rishon le-Zion, Rosh Pinnah and Zikhron Ya'akov were a few of the names which would become synonymous with Jewish pioneering. In 1894 the false accusation of treason against Captain Alfred Dreyfus and the subsequent outbreak of antisemitism in France prompted Theodor Herzl to seek a solution to the Jewish problem. Two years later his *Jewish State* was published and in 1897 the first Zionist Congress met in Basle, and established the World Zionist Movement.

The country's development was stimulated not only from abroad. In 1860 with the completion of Mishkenot Sha'ananim, erected by Sir Moses Montefiore, the Jews of Jerusalem began to move out of the confines of the city's walls. The new quarter was soon joined by others: Nahalat Shiva in 1869, Me'ah She'arim in 1874, Beit David and Beit Ya'akov in 1877. In 1870 the first agricultural school was established at Mikveh Israel. Eight years later the Jews of Jerusalem founded Petah Tikvah which was abandoned, however, shortly thereafter, to be revived later by the immigrants from Russia. New houses, synagogues and public buildings were also erected.

Simultaneously, the Hebrew language which had for centuries been used only for prayer and religious study, was revived as a modern language. Eliezer Ben-Yehuda, who arrived in Palestine in 1881, devoted his life to coining new terms and propagating the daily use of Hebrew. By 1892 both Jewish and general studies were taught in Hebrew in some schools.

Nor did the Zionists confine themselves to rebuilding the land. As part of their effort "to establish a home for the Jewish people in Palestine," Herzl sought the support and assistance of numerous heads of state. In return for an autonomous Jewish Palestine he offered to help the Turkish Sultan solve his financial problems. In 1898 the German Kaiser Wilhelm II came to Jerusalem where the Turks broke a gap in the Old City walls near Jaffa Gate to allow the Emperor's carriage to enter. During his visit, Wilhelm met with Herzl, but later lost whatever interest he may have had in helping the Zionist cause. The Sultan, too, decided against the Zionist proposal, and the Zionists then concentrated on "practical" settlement.

In 1903 a new wave of pogroms in Russia gave impetus to a new wave of immigration. Between 1904 and 1914 some 40,000 persons came to Palestine as part of what is known as the "Second Aliyah." Many returned to Russia or continued on to other countries, disillusioned by the Holy Land or defeated by its many problems and challenges. But those who remained laid the foundations of a new society. In 1909 they established the first kibbutz, or communal settlement, called Deganya. They founded the first Jewish defense organization (Ha-Shomer) to protect the new settlements and fields. They created political parties and established Hebrew as the language of the Jewish community (the Yishuv). In 1909, on the outskirts of Jaffa, they founded a Jewish suburb which later became Tel Aviv. On the eve of the First World War the newcomers accounted for a third of the total Jewish population in the country. Among the leaders of the Second Aliyah were David Ben-Gurion, Yitzhak Ben-Zvi, and Levi Eshkol.

The shot that killed Archduke Franz Ferdinand at Sarajevo in 1914 and plunged the world into global conflict had an almost calamitous effect on Palestine. In December 1914, 700 Jews who were foreign nationals were deported to Egypt. This led to a mass exodus of Jews in the course of which almost 15% of the Jewish population left the country. Large-scale recruitment, heavy taxes, compulsory labor service and the confiscation of food and property, left the population destitute. A locust invasion in 1915–16 added to the misery and poverty. Zionism and all of its manifestations were outlawed. In self-defense, the majority of the remaining Jewish community sought to convince the Turks of their loyalty to the Ottoman cause. A few intrepid Jews, however, managed to contact the British in Egypt and establish a secret intelligence ring. In September 1917 the Nili ring was uncovered by the authorities and its members were arrested.

But as had happened before and would happen again in the course of the country's history, despair was mixed with hope, and defeat with victory. On October 31, 1917, the British opened an attack from their base in Egypt and captured Beersheba, Gaza and Jaffa. On December 11, General Edmund Allenby, Commander-in-Chief of the Egyptian Expeditionary Force, officially entered Jerusalem through the Jaffa Gate. Ottoman rule over the Holy Land ended a little more than 400 years after it had begun; British rule, which was to last almost 30 years, began.

For the Jews the British were more than saviors from Turkish oppression. Shortly before the liberation of Jerusalem, on November 2, 1917, the British Foreign Secretary, Lord Balfour issued his famous declaration stating that the British Government "view with favour the establishment in Palestine of a national home for the Jewish people." The Balfour Declaration was largely the result of efforts by Chaim Weizmann, to secure Allied support for the Zionist cause. Its effect upon the Yishuv and Jewish communities throughout the world was immediate and electrifying.

Although it was not until September 1918 that the British troops occupied the northern portion of the country, a military administration was established in 1917 and ruled Palestine for the next three years. Part of the occupation force was the famed Jewish Legion, two Jewish battalions which grew out of the Zion Mule Corps, and to which was later added a third Palestinian battalion called the Judean Regiment. Nevertheless, the military administration, headed by Sir Ronald Storrs, the British Military Governor of Jerusalem, showed no sympathy for the Zionist cause. It obviously preferred the Sykes-Picot Agreement, which divided the country between the French and the British, to the Balfour Declaration and the aims of the Zionists. At first, the Arabs, to whom the British had also promised independence, were more interested in the Greater Arab State of Syria, Lebanon, Iraq and Saudi Arabia. During this period Hussein, Sharif of Mecca, supported the Zionists. His son, Emir Feisal, on January 3, 1919, signed an agreement with Weizmann calling for "all necessary measures . . . to encourage and stimulate immigration of Jews into Palestine on a large scale, and . . . to settle Jewish immigrants on the soil." Two months later Feisal wrote to the prominent American Zionist, Felix Frankfurter, that "we will wish the Jews a hearty welcome home." Unfortunately, cooperation between Jews and Arabs remained a mere scrap of paper.

On April 24, 1920, the Peace Conference at San Remo agreed to grant Britain the Mandate over Palestine. The boundaries of the country were negotiated between Britain and France and on July 22, 1922, the League of Nations confirmed the Palestine Mandate, citing the language of the Balfour Declaration.

With the end of the military administration, Sir Herbert Samuel was appointed High Commissioner and arrived to take up his new post in July 1920. A few months earlier, in March and April, the Jewish settlements in the upper Galilee were attacked by Arabs and anti-Jewish riots took place in Jerusalem. Samuel attempted an "even-handed" policy. He facilitated the absorption of the Third Aliyah, which began in 1919 and made Hebrew one of the official languages. At the same time he appointed Haj Amin al-Husseini, who had been convicted of inciting the 1920 riots, as Grand Mufti of Jerusalem. The following year, Husseini was elected president of the Supreme Moslem Council. But Samuel's attempts to appease the Arab extremists were not successful. Early in 1921 Feisal's brother Abdullah invaded Transjordan, which had been officially included within the boundaries of the Palestine Mandate. Winston Churchill, British Colonial Secretary, recognized Feisal as emir and subsequently excluded Transjordan from the provisions of the Balfour Declaration. In May of the same year, Arab attacks on Jews in Jaffa, Rehovot, Petah Tikvah and elsewhere left 47 dead and 140 wounded. Samuel responded with a temporary halt to immigration. In June the Churchill White Paper formally instituted limited immigration by establishing immigration certificates, the number of which would be determined by the Government.

The 35,000 immigrants of the Third Aliyah, who arrived between 1919 and 1923, came mainly from Russia and Poland. Most were members of socialist Zionist youth movements, who learned Hebrew and underwent agricultural training before their immigration. They, together with their predecessors, who had founded the Kupat Holim, founded the Histadrut, the General Federation of Jewish Labor, in 1920, as well as its eventual subsidiaries such as the Solel Boneh construction company, the Tnuva agricultural marketing cooperative, Bank Hapoalim, Koor industries and the Hamashbir department stores. Numerous new kibbutzim were established, as was another type of cooperative settlement, the moshav. The Jezreel Valley was purchased by the Jewish National Fund, an arm of the

Zionist Organization. In the wake of the 1920 riots the Haganah, a self-defense organization was established. In April 1920 elections to the Asefat ha-Nivḥarim, the supreme organ of the Yishuv for communal affairs, were held. It, in turn, elected the Va'ad Leumi, or National Council, whose Executive headed various departments and served as the leaders of the Jewish community. Concessions for an electric power plant and Dead Sea potash works were granted to Pinḥas Rutenberg in 1921 and to Moshe Novomeysky in the early thirties, respectively.

In 1924 the Fourth Aliyah began. This time it consisted mainly of middle-class people from Poland, who settled in Palestine's cities and towns, investing their funds in building, factories and shops. The development of the Jezreel Valley continued, as did that of the Coastal Plain, especially Tel Aviv, and the Sharon Valley. In 1925 the Hebrew University was opened on Mount Scopus. The Haifa Technion had been inaugurated. Hebrew newspapers, books and theater were flourishing, and a Hebrew school system was supported by the Zionist Executive. In 1927 Asefat ha-Nivḥarim was recognized by the British authorities as the official representatives of the Yishuv.

The relative peace which existed since 1921 was shattered in 1929 by a new outbreak of Arab violence. A dispute over the Western Wall was used by the Mufti of Jerusalem to incite the Arabs against the Jews. Although the Haganah repulsed the attacks in Jerusalem, 70 Jews were killed in Hebron and 18 in Safed. Most were old men, women and children. As a result of the subsequent commission of inquiry, a White Paper was issued which further curtailed Jewish immigration and settlement. But in the face of public pressure and Weizmann's resignation as Chairman of the Jewish Agency, the British backed down.

Four years later, in 1933, Hitler came to power in Germany. The small number of immigrants of the Fifth Aliyah, which began in 1929, swelled and nearly 165,000 Jews entered the country legally between 1933 and 1936. Thousands of others seeking refuge from the Nazis came "illegally", without immigration certificates. The total Jewish population of Palestine in 1936 reached 400,000, a third of the total, with 150,000 in Tel Aviv, 76,000 in Jerusalem (60% of the city's inhabitants) and 50,000 in Haifa (about half of the city's population).

In April 1936 the three year "Arab Rebellion" broke out. The Arab Higher Committee headed by the Mufti, demanded an end to Jewish immigration and to the transfer of land to Jews. It backed its demand with a general strike and attacks on Jews throughout the country. Although the strike ended within six months, the violence continued. All told, nearly 500 Jews were killed. The British again sent a commission of inquiry and in July 1937 the Royal Commission, headed by Lord Peel, issued a report calling for the partition of Palestine into a Jewish and an Arab state, with Jerusalem remaining in the hands of the British.

The rebellion was crushed by British troops by the spring of 1939, but in May of that year the MacDonald White Paper restricted Jewish immigration to 10,000 a year for the next five years, with immigration thereafter dependent on Arab consent. The sale of land to Jews was again sharply curtailed. After the outbreak of World War II only a few months later, the Yishuv refused to accept Britain's attempt to lock the door in the face of the escapees from the Nazi terror. David Ben-Gurion announced that the Jews "would fight Hitler as if there were no White Paper and would fight the White Paper as if there were no Hitler."

During the Arab rebellion, the Haganah took upon itself the responsibility for the safety of Jewish settlements. In cooperation with the British, Special Night Squads were set up composed of Haganah members and British troops. They were led and trained by Captain Orde Wingate and used guerrilla tactics to fight the terrorists. Jewish supernumerary and settlement police units were also established. But this "recognition" by the British did not prevent the Haganah from maintaining its underground forces and promoting the illegal immigration known as Aliyah Bet. At the same time, another underground organization, the Irgun Ẓeva'i Le'umi or IZL, which had split from the Haganah, began to operate against the Mandatory authorities.

Although thousands of Palestinian Jews volunteered to join the British war effort, the latter were reluctant to accept them. Moreover, the Government continued to refuse entry to refugees from Europe, even deporting some. It was not until mid-1940 that Jewish volunteers were accepted in the British Army and not until September 1944 that a Jewish Brigade was established. When the German threat to the Middle East became serious, members of the Haganah were asked to volunteer for special

8

missions in cooperation with the British, but as the threat receded, the Government again confiscated the underground's arms and imprisoned those caught possessing them.

Early in 1944, the IZL, headed by Menachem Begin, declared a revolt against the British, attacking Government installations in an effort to persuade the British to leave the country. In November 1944, the British Minister of State, Lord Moyne was killed by members of LEHI, another underground organization, which accused him of responsibility for refusing refuge to European Jews. Nor did the end of the war in 1945, or the election of the British Labor Party, change the situation. The gates of the country were kept locked and, in response, illegal immigration was stepped up and the three underground organizations united to form the Jewish Resistance Movement.

Although unity between the Jewish underground forces lasted less than a year, the struggle against the British continued through 1946 and 1947. The British, on their part, intensified their search for arms and Jewish resistance fighters, arrested Jewish leaders, interned or deported illegal immigrants, and gradually retreated into armed compounds established throughout the country.

Early in 1947, exhausted by the struggle against Germany, weary of the bloodletting in Palestine, economically unable to bear the cost of maintaining its troops in the Holy Land, Britain turned the Palestine problem over to the newly-formed United Nations, perhaps in the hope that the UN would back its position. The UN sent a Special Commission (UNSCOP) to investigate the situation in both Palestine and the Displaced Persons camps in Europe. A majority of the UNSCOP members recommended the partition of Palestine into a Jewish and an Arab state with economic union, with Jerusalem as an international city. On November 29, 1947 the United Nations General Assembly accepted the Partition Plan.

But while the Jews announced their acceptance of the UN decision, the British stated that they would not cooperate in its implementation and the Arab states proclaimed their determination to go to war to prevent it from being carried out. Arab violence began immediately. With the support of the Arab states, local bands and volunteers from across the border attacked Jewish settlements and towns. The British, for the most part, stood on the sidelines.

At first the Jewish community, numbering some 600,000, was hard-pressed. Villages in the Galilee and the Negev were isolated; the Ezyon Bloc in the Hebron Hills fell; Jerusalem was besieged and the Jewish Quarter in the Old City was under heavy attack and surrendered. But gradually the underground organized into an army, arms were secured from abroad, air, naval and artillery units were created.

On May 14, 1948 the last British troops left the country and in an emotional ceremony in the Tel Aviv Museum, David Ben-Gurion read the Declaration of Independence establishing the State of Israel.

That same evening the Arab States surrounding Israel attacked the fledgling state. Nevertheless, the Israel Defense Forces (IDF) gradually began to make headway. The way to Jerusalem was opened through an alternate route, Safed and the Galilee were in Jewish hands and the Egyptian forces in the Negev were forced to retreat. A cease-fire was called for by the Security Council, but when it expired fighting began anew. This time, however, Israel's victory was decisive. By the beginning of 1949, Israel's army controlled the entire Galilee and the Negev, the Coastal Plain up to Gaza and the new city of Jerusalem with a corridor connecting it to the rest of the country. The Arabs, on the other hand, had captured the Old City of Jerusalem, the Jordanian Army held most of Judea and Samaria and the Egyptian Army controlled the Gaza Strip.

Between February and July 1949 Israel negotiated and signed armistice agreements with Egypt, Jordan and Syria on the island of Rhodes, with the assistance of UN Mediator Ralph Bunche. The end of armed conflict did not, however, bring peace between Israel and its Arab neighbors. The thousands of Palestinian Arabs who fled from their homes in fear and at the urging of their leaders, despite Israeli attempts to persuade them to stay, became a pawn in the hands of those Arabs who refused to recognize Israel's right to exist. Some were trained as terrorists and sent to attack the new state. Jordan refused to honor its commitments to give the Jews access to their Holy Places in the Old City of Jerusalem. The Hebrew University and Hadassah Hospital on Mount Scopus were isolated and made unusable. The Syrians continued to harass the settlers in the Galilee who lay within range of their guns, and the Egyptians supported terror as a means to continue the war they had lost.

9

Israel had other problems as well. As soon as the State was declared its gates were thrown open to the survivors of the Nazi Holocaust, as well as to Jews in communities throughout North Africa and the Middle East. By the end of 1948, more than 100,000 Jews had entered the new state. Another 584,000 arrived in the next three years. Their absorption was a gigantic effort for Israel. Overcrowded temporary camps were established, food was short and rationing was introduced, unemployment was widespread.

But with the aid of foreign assistance from the United States, contributions from Jews living abroad and a controversial reparations agreement signed with Germany in September 1952, the country began to emerge from its economic bind. New kibbutzim, moshavim and towns were established (345 between 1948 and 1951), roads and houses were built, large-scale development projects, such as the draining of the Huleh swamps, were begun, the El Al national airline was established, and government corporations were created to exploit Israel's natural resources.

At the same time, political institutions were organized. Dr. Chaim Weizmann was elected President and David Ben-Gurion Prime Minister. General elections to the country's parliament, the Knesset, gave a plurality to the Labor Party. Israel was recognized by the Soviet Union and the United States and was admitted to the United Nations.

There was, however, still no peace along the borders. From 1951 to 1956 more than 400 Israelis were killed and 900 wounded by Arab infiltrators and terrorists. The Arabs instituted a boycott of Israel and blockaded the Gulf of Eilat. By 1956 terrorism in the south had reached unbearable proportions. A year earlier Egypt's President Nasser had signed the first arms pact in the region with Russia. When Egypt, Syria and Jordan joined in a military pact against Israel, the IDF reacted. On October 29, 1956, Israel moved into the Sinai Desert quickly overrunning Egyptian positions there and in the Gaza Strip, and reached the bank of the Suez Canal. Britain and France, in an attempt to regain control of the recently nationalized Canal, joined the conflict and bombarded Egyptian positions along the Canal. The United Nations, led by the United States and Russia called for a cease-fire and withdrawal by British, French and Israeli forces. In 1957 Israel complied after being assured that UN troops stationed at Sharm el-Sheikh would keep the sea route to Eilat open.

The new trade route to Asia and Africa opened a gap in the hostile ring which surrounded Israel. New relationships and close ties were established with numerous African and Asian countries to whom Israel supplied technical assistance.

In 1958 Israel celebrated its tenth anniversary. During that first decade the population had grown to over two million (of which 940,000 were immigrants), the land under cultivation had been increased by 150%, a road had been paved from Beersheba to Eilat where a port was beginning to be built. Industry had doubled its output, unemployment had fallen to 1.4%, half a million pupils attended schools.

Two years later Israel looked back to the past. Adolf Eichmann, a key official in the Nazi murder of six million Jews, was captured by Israeli agents and placed on trial in Jerusalem. The prolonged trial of "the man in the glass booth" served to educate Israeli youth and the world on the bestiality of man. He was hanged in 1962.

During the following years Israel continued to progress and develop in numerous areas. The new Hadassah Medical Center was opened in Jerusalem, as was the Israel Museum; an archeological team under Prof. Yiga'el Yadin discovered Bar Kochba's letters in the Judean Desert; an atomic reactor was built at Nahal Soreq; a new port was built in Ashdod; the new Knesset building was opened; Shmuel Yosef Agnon received the Nobel Prize for Literature.

On the political scene, Yizhak Ben-Zvi, who had replaced Weizmann as President, died and was succeeded by Zalman Shazar; David Ben-Gurion resigned as Prime Minister and was replaced by Levi Eshkol; Israel and West Germany agreed to establish diplomatic relations.

Then, in May 1967, with Egypt's movement of troops into Sinai, the constant Arab attacks turned into the threat of full-scale war. Nasser ordered the UN troops out of Sharm el-Sheikh and reimposed the blockade of the Gulf of Eilat. As the nations of the world failed to respond to this blatant disregard for international guarantees, Israel's friends were gripped with fear for its safety and both volunteers and aid came pouring into the country. On June 5th Israel executed a pre-emptive air strike which destroyed Arab air power on the ground. In the next six days, the IDF routed the Egyptians, capturing the Gaza Strip and Sinai and reaching (once again) the banks of the Suez Canal. In the north, the

Syrians were chased off the Golan Heights after a bitter battle, and on the east, Israeli forces took all the land up to the Jordan River, returning to such ancient sites as the Old City and Western Wall in Jerusalem, the Ezyon Bloc, Hebron and Jericho.

On June 27th the Government of Israel announced the annexation of Jerusalem, declaring that the walls which had divided the city for nearly two decades would never again be erected. It insisted that the Six Day War was a purely defensive one and that it had no intention of retaining the territory it had captured. If the Arabs would agree to make peace, it declared, almost all the territory would be returned. In August the Arab Summit Conference at Khartoum delivered its reply: "No peace, no recognition and no negotiations with Israel."

Despite this Arab stand, Israel established an "Open Bridges" policy for Judea and Samaria, allowing the free movement of persons and goods across the border. It also instituted a liberal occupation policy, allowing for free municipal and local elections.

The following year, in September 1968, Egypt began massive artillery attacks across the cease-fire line. The fighting escalated into the War of Attrition, with Israel building the Bar-Lev Line on the Canal to protect its troops and responding to the Egyptian bombardments with its own air raids deep into Egypt. In August 1970 an American initiated cease-fire went into effect.

Meanwhile, terrorist attacks began again. Civilian aircrafts were hijacked. In 1972 eleven Israeli athletes were murdered at the Munich Olympics and a group of Japanese terrorists machinegunned 27 passengers to death at Ben-Gurion Airport. In 1974, 24 schoolchildren were murdered by terrorists at a school in northern Israel.

Prime Minister Levi Eshkol died in 1969 and was succeeded by Golda Meir. Immigration increased beginning in 1970 with an influx of newcomers both from the Western countries and the Soviet Union.

On October 6, 1973, Egypt and Syria launched a surprise two-front attack on Israel. The Bar-Lev Line was quickly overrun and Syrian forces almost reached the bridges over the Jordan. But, with the help of a massive American arms air lift, the Israeli forces recovered, crossed the west bank of the Suez Canal and surrounded the Second and Third Egyptian Armies, and recaptured the Golan Heights in the north, coming to a halt some 20 miles from Damascus.

Following the cease-fire, which went into effect on October 24th, U.S. Secretary of State, Henry Kissinger, negotiated an agreement between Egypt and Israel for the exchange of prisoners of war and the release of the beleaguered Third Army. Details of the agreement were worked out in direct negotiations between the two sides at Kilometer 101 of the Suez–Cairo road. One month later, on December 21st, representatives of Egypt, Israel and Jordan met under the joint chairmanship of the United States and Russia at the Geneva Peace Conference. Although the conference adjourned the following day, it laid the groundwork for the separation of forces agreement between Egypt and Israel, signed in January 1974 and fully implemented two months later. After numerous efforts, Kissinger was finally able to bring about a similar agreement between Syria and Israel on May 31st, 1974. In September 1975, Egypt and Israel signed an interim agreement under which Israel withdrew even further from the Suez Canal, giving up the strategic Mitla and Gidi passes and the Abu Rodeis oilfields.

Within Israel, the large number of casualties in the 1973 war and the fact that the nation was caught by surprise, led to a feeling of depression and sharp criticism of the government. Nevertheless, the ruling Labor Party won a renewed mandate to form a coalition government in December 1973. The following year, however, Prime Minister Golda Meir resigned and was replaced by Yizhak Rabin, who appointed new cabinet ministers.

In 1975, the Suez Canal was reopened and an Israeli-bound cargo passed through it. Since 1967 over 100,000 immigrants from the Soviet Union arrived in the country. A trade agreement was signed between Israel and the European Economic Community. Prices continued to rise and successive devaluations lowered the value of the Israeli pound.

Terrorist attacks continued and, in 1976, Israeli troops staged a dramatic rescue of over 100 hostages held by terrorist hijackers at Uganda's Entebbe airport. The same year, the "Good Fence" was opened on the Israel-Lebanese border, allowing victims of the civil war between Christians and Moslems to seek medical aid in Israel, Lebanese farmers to sell crops in Israel, and Lebanese workers to find employment in Israel. Israel also supplied water to villages in Lebanon cut off by the war, provided agricultural extension courses, and allowed Lebanese teachers to visit Israeli schools.

11

In December 1976 the Rabin Government resigned and new parliamentary elections were set for May 1977. On that date, in an unexpected move, the Israeli public swept the Labor Party from office. For the first time since the Va'ad Leumi elections, Labor was no longer the party which formed the government. Menachem Begin, heading a Likud coalition, was elected Prime Minister after eight unsuccessful attempts to obtain that post.

The new Prime Minister appointed Moshe Dayan as Foreign Minister, with the latter leaving Labor to accept the position. Begin traveled to the United States to meet President Carter, visited Rumania, offered aid to the embattled Christians in southern Lebanon, and gave sanctuary to 66 Vietnamese refugees rescured by an Israeli ship in South East Asia.

Begin, as each preceding Prime Minister before him, also extended an invitation to the heads of the surrounding Arab States to meet with him and negotiate an Arab-Israeli peace agreement. In November 1977, Egyptian President Anwar Sadat dramatically announced his intention to come to Jerusalem to meet Israeli leaders and address the Knesset. This meeting was followed by the Cairo Conference and by Begin's trip to Ismailia and negotiations between Arabs and Israelis in both Cairo and Jerusalem.

Thus, 130 years after the first picture of the Holy Land emerged, a new image is slowly being formed — one of peace and cooperation, rather than violence and turmoil. The past is clear, the future less certain, but, as the history of the land and its people portrayed on the following pages shows us, hope lies ahead.

12

ILLUSTRATION CREDITS

"If you will, it is no dream"
Theodor Herzl

1. The Menorah, symbol of the State of Israel, stands opposite the Knesset building in Jerusalem. 2. The Shrine of the Book, in the foreground, and the Knesset building. 3. The reconstructed arks in the Rabbi Johanan ben-Zakkai's synagogue in the Old City of Jerusalem.

1. Herod's temple, as depicted in the reconstruction of Jerusalem during the second temple period at the Holy Land Hotel, Jerusalem.

2. Damascus Gate, the most magnificent and busiest of all gates to the Old City of Jerusalem. Within the walls one can see, at the left, the tower of the Lutheran Church of the Redemption, and the large dome of the Church of the Holy Sepulcher.

1. The 16th century walls of the Old City of Jerusalem. One can almost circumvent the entire city by walking on top of the parapet.

2. Aerial view of the Old City of Jerusalem, looking south. In the foreground is the Rockefeller Museum of Archeology.

1

2

The crusader castle of Monfort, in the Western Galilee, was one of the many crusader relics in the Holy Land.

The Arabah Valley, in the southern part of the country, is a natural hot-house for out-of-season agricultural products. The Red Sea is an underwater fairy land of fish and corals, and a paradise for skin-divers.

The Galilee, in the northern part of Israel, has many mountain villages, like this one of Peki'in. In Tiberias, on Lake Kinneret, is the traditional and venerated tomb of Rabbi Meir Ba'al ha-Nes.

Tabor oaks in the Ḥurshat Tal National Park in Upper Galilee. View of the Dead Sea, world's lowest point, and the Moab plateau on its eastern side.

1. Since 1967, more than 150,000 immigrants have come from the Soviet Union to make their new homes in Israel. 2. Newly arrived Moroccan immigrants awaiting their disembarkation at Haifa Port. Most of the Jews from North Africa have immigrated to Israel.

1. Yeshiva students, studying in pairs, in order to develop their power of articulate reasoning.

3. A chemistry class at the Hebrew University Givat Ram campus in Jerusalem.

2. A Hebrew University geology class on a field trip in the Negev.

4. Vocational training at Neurim School of Youth Aliyah.

1. A scribe writing a Torah scroll. The scribe is a professional expert, known in Hebrew as *sofer setam, setam* being the Hebrew initials of *Sefer Torah, tefillin,* and *mezuzot.* These are written on specially prepared parchment, in straight lines, with a feather quill in indelible ink.

2. The Dead Sea scrolls on exhibit at the Hebrew University, Jerusalem, before they were transferred to their permanent show-place in the Shrine of the Book at the Israel Museum. The first scrolls were discovered by chance in 1947, and were first recognized as authentic by Prof. Sukenik. They date mostly from the end of the Second Temple period, and consist of biblical texts, Apocrypha and Pseudoepigraphia books. as well as community documents.

1

2

The main reading room of the Jewish National and University Library at the Hebrew University, Givat Ram campus, Jerusalem

1

2

Hebrew Book Week, an annual open-air book fair held all over Israel.

1. A shofar-maker in Haifa, one of the few who still practice this ancient craft, making different shofars according to each community's traditions.

2. A Yemenite Jew blowing a spiral Yemenite shofar at the Western Wall in Jerusalem.

3. "Kapparot" ceremony, Safed, 1972. The father is waving a fowl around the head of his son as a substitute; "the fowl will go to its death, and I shall enter a good and long life and peace".

4. Celebrating the feast of Tabernacles—Sukkot—in an ornate sukkah of a Jerusalem family of Persian origin.

1. Scouts taking part in the ceremonial kindling of the Hannukah torch at Modi'in. The torch is relayed by runners from the site of the Maccabean tombs to Jerusalem.

2. Kindling at sundown the individual torches which form a Hannukah menorah near the Western Wall, Jerusalem.

3. Tree planting, a tradition carried out by school children on Tu-bi-Shevat, the New Year for Trees.

1. A float, part of the *Adloyada* Purim carnival procession held in Tel Aviv.

2. A Jerusalem family of Persian origin, is gathered around the Seder table, beginning the weeklong celebration of Passover.

1. Tanks in formation passing by Jerusalem's Old City wall during Israel's 25th anniversary parade.

2. Dancing and merry-making in Jerusalem's Zion Square on the eve of Israel's 25th Independence Day, 1973.

3. Ḥasidim dancing around the Lag ba-Omer bonfire at Meron, traditional tomb of Rabbi Simeon bar Yoḥai.

1. Symbolic reaping of the omer at one of the kibbutzim, in which the first ripe grain of the season is harvested.

2. Jerusalem children bringing the season's first fruit, as part of the Shavuot celebration, thus following an ancient tradition of bringing fruit to the sanctuary.

3. The Western Wall on the night of Tishah be-Av.

1

2
Views of Jerusalem by an unknown photographer, 1847: 1. The Dome of the Rock. 2. The Citadel of David.

The Wailing Wall in Jerusalem, by J. Robertson and A. Beato, c. 1857.

1

2

1. The building above Rachel's tomb near Bethlehem, which was renovated in 1841 with funds given by Sir Moses Montefiore. 2. Inside the Tomb.

Bilu

1. A publicity photograph for the vineyards of Rishon le-Zion, c. 1897. 2. The first locomotive for the railroad between Jaffa and Jerusalem, constructed 1890–92.
3. Yesud ha-Ma'alah in the Huleh valley, founded in 1883 by settlers from the Polish town of Mezhirech.

5

6

Nationalbibliothek in Jerusalem und deren Gründer Dr. J. Chasanowicz

הספריה הלאומית בירושלים ומיסדה ד״ר י. חזנוביץ

7

4. The Erez Israel pavilion at the Berlin World Fair of 1896. The pavilion was managed by Moshe David Schub (Figure 5), one of the founders of Rosh Pinna
6. The Midrash Abrabanel library founded in 1892 in Jerusalem, to which the collection of Joseph Chasanowich (inset) was later added. 7. Misgav Ladach, Jewi
hospital in the Old City of Jerusalem, founded in 1889.

1

2

1. The Kaiser and his party riding past the Yemin Moshe quarter of Jerusalem. In the background is the wall of the Old City and the Citadel of David. 2. A triumphal arch erected on Jaffa Road in honor of the Kaiser's visit. The inscriptions in Hebrew and German read: "Blessed be he who comes in the name of the Lord; We bless you from the house of the Lord."

1

2

1. Theodor Herzl visited Ereẓ Israel in 1898 to meet the Kaiser there. Here he is visiting Reḥovot, where he was enthusiastically received. 2. Herzl (dressed in white, standing in the doorway) at the home of the Stern family on Mamilla Road. It was here that he stayed during his visit to Jerusalem (Oct. 28–Nov. 3, 1898).

1

2

3

1. The volunteer fire brigade of Zikhron Ya'akov, c. 1900. The brigade was established in 1897 in the wake of a fire in the wine cellars. 2. The Rishon le-Zion orchestra, c. 1900. It was founded in 1896, having 28 members under the directorship of Boris Ossowetzky. 3. Loading barrels of wine onto camels at the Rishon le-Zion cellar for export through the port of Jaffa, c. 1900.

4

5

6

4. Kefar Saba, c. 1910; founded in 1903 by First Aliyah immigrants. 5. Teachers and pupils of a Talmud Torah in Hebron, 1902. 6. The Schneller orphanage in Jerusalem, c. 1900. The orphanage was founded in 1860 by Ludwig Schneller, a German Protestant, for Syrian orphans.

1. An American Christian family on a pilgrimage to Ereẓ Israel, 1907. 2. Bustrus Street in Jaffa, 1908. This was the year that Arthur Ruppin settled in Ereẓ Israel and opened the Palestine Office on Bustrus Street. (A flag is flying from the second story balcony.) 3. Atid, edible oil and soap factory, founded by Naḥum Wilbush (Wilbuschewitz) at Bet Arif (later Ben Shemen) near Lydda, 1906.

1. Laying the foundation stone for Tel Aviv (Aḥuzzat Bayit) during the intermediate days of Sukkot, 1908. 2. The Fourth Convention of Ha-Po'el ha-Ẓa'ir labor movement in Jaffa, 1908.

1

2

3

1. Transporting the grain from the threshing floor, Gederah, 1910. 2. The Palestine Office training farm for agricultural workers at Ben Shemen, c. 1910. 3. Harvesting early grapes at Rishon le-Zion, a publicity photo, 1910.

6

. The original mud hut of Deganyah Alef, with Joseph Baratz standing in front of it, 1910. 5. Watchmen by their watchtower in Rishon le-Zion, c. 1912. 6. An
utdoor oven in a settlement, c. 1910. 7. The Kevuẓat Kinneret courtyard, 1910.

1

2

3

1. Herzl Street, Tel Aviv. The Herzlia Gymnasium can be seen at the end of the street. (Photo, Leo Kann, 1910–11.) 2. Sports lesson at the Herzlia Gymnasiur. At the right is the sports teacher Zevi Nishri. (Photo, Leo Kann, 1910–11.) 3. The Herzlia Gymnasium. Seated on the donkey is Dr. H. Hisin, one of the founde of Ahuzzat Bayit and the physician of "little Tel Aviv."

6

The committee for the suburb of Tel Aviv, on the front porch of Meir Dizengoff's house. On the sidewalk are the neighborhood guards; photo, 1911. 5. The ulamit Conservatoire founded in 1910 by Selma (Shulamit) Ruppin. The conductor is the noted violinist Hopenko. 6. Soldiers quelling the riotous crowd outside Church of the Holy Sepulcher in Jerusalem during the Greek Orthodox Holy Fire ceremony.

בטול האסור עד כותל המערבי

ביום הששי בבוקר קבלנו מסופרנו המיוחד בקושטא, מר ב. ר. את הודיעה התשובה הזאת,
שנדפסה בהוספה מיוחדה :

1. Eliezer Ben-Yehuda. The first volume of his Hebrew dictionary was published in 1910. 2. The editorial board of *Ha-Aḥdut*, the Hebrew newspaper of Po'ale Zion. L. to R.: Izḥak Ben-Zvi, Jacob Zerubavel, David Ben-Gurion, and Raḥel Yannait (Ben-Zvi). 3. A headline from the Jerusalem Newspaper *Ha-Ḥerut* (Feb. 11, 1912) announcing that the Turkish restrictions on bringing benches and candles to the Western Wall had been revoked. 4. Jews praying at the Western Wall, 1912.

6

8

5. Ostriches in Reḥovot, 1912. They were brought to Ereẓ Israel by the zoologist Israel Aharoni for use of their plumage in the fashion industry. 6. A stream near the moshavah Migdal in the Ginossar Valley, c. 1912. 7. A Yemenite teacher and pupils in the Naḥaliel quarter of Haderah, 1912. 8. The 1912 agricultural fair in Reḥovot.

1

2
1. Graduates of preparatory schools and teachers seminary in Jerusalem and Tel Aviv who enlisted in Turkish army, Passover 1916. 2. Jamal Pasha, head of the Turkish military administration in Erez Israel, visiting Rishon le-Zion, April 1916.

3

4

5

Jewish soldiers in the Austrian army visiting the Western Wall in 1915. During World War I there were 275,000 Jewish soldiers in the Austro-Hungarian army. 5. About 12,000 Jews were deported by the Turks to Egypt from Erez Israel during 1915. Figure 4 shows a group of refugees leaving Erez Israel and Figure 5 ows them arriving in Egypt.

1

2
1. A convoy of Turkish troops in Erez Israel, 1914. 2. Soldiers of the Zion Mule Corps in Egypt, 1915.

David Ben-Gurion, c. 1913–14, when he was a law student in Constantinople. Ben-Gurion said "The settlement of the land is the only true Zionism, all else being ⸺f-deception, empty verbiage, and merely a pastime." 4. Aharon David Gordon (1856–1922), Hebrew writer and spiritual mentor of that wing of the Zionist labor ⸺ovement which emphasized self-realization through settlement on the land. 5. Soldiers of the Jewish Legion in Erez Israel, 1917.

1917

Foreign Office,
November 2nd, 1917.

Dear Lord Rothschild,

I have much pleasure in conveying to you, on behalf of His Majesty's Government, the following declaration of sympathy with Jewish Zionist aspirations which has been submitted to, and approved by, the Cabinet.

"His Majesty's Government view with favour the establishment in Palestine of a national home for the Jewish people, and will use their best endeavours to facilitate the achievement of this object, it being clearly understood that nothing shall be done which may prejudice the civil and religious rights of existing non-Jewish communities in Palestine, or the rights and political status enjoyed by Jews in any other country".

I should be grateful if you would bring this declaration to the knowledge of the Zionist Federation.

1. British army tank. 2. The Balfour Declaration. 3. The mayor of Jerusalem (with cane) surrenders the city to two British privates. 4. British guard at the Grotto of Nativity, Bethlehem. 5. General Allenby enters the Old City of Jerusalem on foot.

Chaim Weizmann with Emir Feisal. 2. Vladimir (Ze'ev) Jabotinsky. 3. Insignia of the Jewish Legion. 4. Jewish Legion souvenir album. 5. David Ben-Gurion. 6. Members of the wish Legion visit the Western Wall.

1919

1. Third Aliyah immigrants. 2. Military cemetery on Mount Scopus. 3. Heads of some of the Christian communities. 4. Temporary camp for road-construction workers. 5. Ḥalutzim constructing road.

TO THE PEOPLE OF PALESTINE

The Allied Powers whose Arms were victorious in the late War have entrusted to My Country a Mandate to watch over the interests of Palestine and to ensure to your Country that peaceful and prosperous development which has so long been denied to you.

I recall with pride the large part played by My troops under the command of Field Marshal Lord Allenby in freeing your Country from Turkish rule, and I shall indeed rejoice if I and My people can also be the instruments of bringing within your reach the blessings of a wise and liberal administration.

I desire to assure you of the absolute impartiality with which the duties of the Mandatory Power will be carried out, and of the determination of My Government to respect the rights of every race and every creed represented among you, both for the period which has still to elapse before the terms of the Mandate can be finally approved by the League of Nations, and in the future when the Mandate has become an accomplished fact.

You are well aware that the Allied and Associated Powers have decided that measures shall be adopted to secure the gradual establishment in Palestine of a National Home for the Jewish People. These measures will not in any way affect the civil or religious rights or diminish the prosperity of the general population of Palestine.

The High Commissioner whom I have appointed to carry out these principles will, I am confident, do so whole-heartedly and effectively, and will endeavour to promote in every possible way the welfare and unity of all classes and sections among you.

I realise profoundly the solemnity of the trust involved in the government of a Country which is sacred alike to Christian, Mohammedan, and Jew, and I shall watch with deep interest and warm sympathy the future progress and development of a State whose history has been of such tremendous import to the World.

GEORGE R. and I.

HEADQUARTERS,
OCCUPIED ENEMY TERRITORY ADMINISTRATION (SOUTH),
JERUSALEM.

30. 6. 20.

Handed over to
Sir Herbert Samuel,
one Palestine, complete —

L. J. Bols.
Major General

1. The Proclamation of the British Mandate. 2. An immigrant camp in Tel Aviv. 3. Sir Herbert Samuel, First British High Commissioner to Palestine. 4. The military governor's delivery note to Herbert Samuel. 5. Hajj Amin al-Husseini instigated the riots. 6. Tel Ḥai. 7. The funeral of the heroes of Tel Ḥai.

1921

1. Cairo conference with Winston Churchill. 2. Henrietta Szold with first graduates of Hadassah Nursing School, Jerusalem. 3. Kibbutz Kiryat Anavim. 4. Joseph Ḥayyim Brenner wa killed in riots. Here with wife. 5. Rabbi Abraham Isaac ha-Kohen Kook, Chief Ashkenazi Rabbi. 6. Rabbi Ya'akov Meir, Chief Sephardi Rabbi. 7. En Ḥarod.

1922

אליעזר בן־יהורה
תריח׳ - תרפ״ג

1. Emir Abdullah, second from right, Herbert Samuel, center, and T. E. Lawrence on his right. 2. 40th anniversary of arrival of Bilu in Erez Israel. 3. Eliezer Ben-Yehudah on his death bed. 4. Zev Vilnay with tourists in Jerusalem. 5. One of the many swamps. 6. Plan of Kefar Yehezkel.

1923

1. Albert Einstein visits Palestine. 2. Palestine Opera founded; Rina Nikova and David Brainin in Swan Lake. 3. Porters and drivers at Jerusalem railway station. 4. The Grand Moulin flour mills, Haifa. 5. Constructing a new quarter in Tel Aviv. 6. Women plowing.

1. Fourth Aliyah immigrants from Poland. 2. Tel Aviv. 3. Orthodox children in newly founded Bene Berak. 4. Kefar Ḥasidim—plowing the fields. 5. Kefar Ḥasidim—the synagogue.
6. En Ḥarod in the Jezreel Valley.

1925

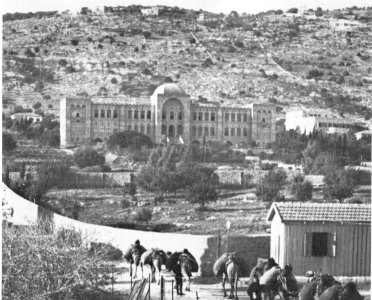

1. Lord Plumer, Second High Commissioner. 2. Unemployed demonstrate in Ḥaderah. 3. Leader of Aḥdut ha-Avodah. left to right, sitting: Ben-Zvi, Ben-Gurion, standing: Katznelson, Rubashov (Shazar). 4. Archeological excavations reveal Jerusalem Third Wall. 5. The Technion opens in Haifa. 6. The Hebrew University in Jerusalem is officially opened.

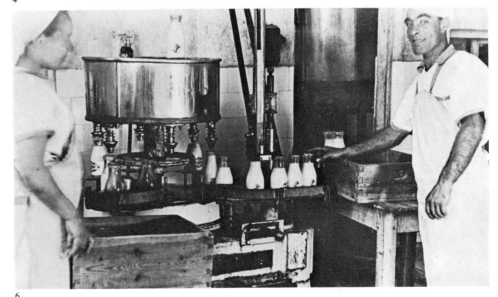

1. "Halutzim" on the Afulah road. 2. Hayyim Naḥman Bialik. 3. Concert in the Citadel of David, Jerusalem. 4. Dagestani Jews demonstrating against British for preventing their enlising in the Transjordan Frontier Force. 5. Nahalal, the first "moshav ovedim". 6. A milk-bottling plant.

1927

1. Thomas Masaryk visiting Jerusalem, escorted by Rabbi Sonnenfeld. 2. Distributing pasteurized milk in Jerusalem. 3. A carpet-weaving workshop. 4. Cornerstone-laying ceremony of Nathan Straus Health Center in Jerusalem. R. to L. Straus, Lord and Lady Plumer. 5. Citrus grove. 6. A colonist from Sejera, with his Jewish laborers.

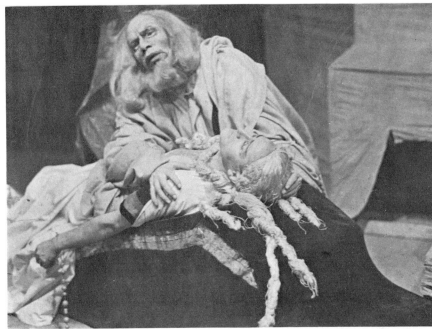

1. Maḥaneh Israel, religious settlement, near Mount Tabor. 2. Unemployed. 3. The Western Wall. 4. Habimah Theater visits Palestine. 5. Construction of the hydroelectric power plant at Naharayim. 6. Road repairs in Tel Aviv.

1929

1. A Hebronite, under guard, packs for evacuation to Jerusalem. 2. Riots against Jews in Hebron. 3. Safed house after Arab attack. 4. Common grave for six Jews killed in Tel Aviv. 5. Fifth Aliyah begins. 6. Betar members on guard duty at Western Wall on 9th of Av.

1. Workers picketing in Kefar Saba for employment of Jewish labor. 2. Chaim Weizmann. 3. Tel Aviv police force joins the country-wide force. 4. British band in front of Hotel Fast, Jerusalem. 5. The Jewish National Library building on Mount Scopus. 6. The King David Hotel in Jerusalem.

1931

1

2

3

4

5

6

7

8

9

1. Chaim Arlosoroff, head of Jewish Agency Political Dept. 2. Arthur Wauchope, center, becomes third British High Commissioner. 3. Nahum Sokolow, elected president of Zionist Organization. 4. Government House, seat of British High Commissioner, completed. 5. Excavations began in Samaria. 6. Palestine Potash Co. Ltd. established at Dead Sea. 7. Carnallite salt transported from pans to processing plant. 8. Secret arms factory of the Haganah in Tel Aviv. 9. Hefer Plain settlers resting after draining swamps.

1. The Jewish Quarter, Jerusalem's Old City. 2. The newly built Jewish Agency Compound. 3. The first Maccabiah, Tel Aviv. 4. The Palestine Post was founded.

1933

1. Police dispersing Arab rioters in Jaffa during the Arab general strike. 2. The YMCA building, Jerusalem. 3. Haifa Port is officially opened. 4. Kiryat Ḥayyim residential quarter in Haifa Bay. 5. Kefar Vitkin founded by veteran agricultural workers. 6. Yossele Rosenblatt, the famous ḥazzan came to Palestine. 7. Arab rioters in Jerusalem.

1. Daniel Sieff Research Institute in Rehovot is founded. 2. Youth Aliyah begins. 3. Jaffa Port. 4. The first steam power station, Haifa. 5. Temporary camp of Youth Aliyah immigrants.
6. The Levant Fair in Tel Aviv. 7. German new immigrants on road construction in Tel Aviv.

1935

1. Ben-Gurion at 19th Zionist Congress in Basle. 2. The Basle Congress Hall. 3. Menahem Mendel Ussishkin, head of JNF, with Y. Foerder, of Rassco. 4. Henrietta Szold with Youth Aliyah children. 5. Tel Aviv beach. 6. Naḥalat Binyamin street, Tel Aviv.

2

4

6

8

1. Arturo Toscanini conducting first concert of Palestine Symphony Orchestra. 2. Kibbutz Hazorea founded. 3. Leveling sand dunes in Haifa bay area. 4. Lord Peel, head of the Peel Commission, at British War Cemetery, Mount Scopus. 5. Tel Aviv harbor opened. 6. Y. L. Magnés (right), one of the founders of Brit Shalom movement. 7. Nahalal. 8. The Levant Fair, Tel Aviv.

1937

1. First roll-call of IZL after split. 2. Power line for 60,000 volts built from Naharayim to Tel Aviv. 3. Yizhak Sadeh, commander & creator of *(peluggot sadeh)* Field Squads. 4. The British District Commissioner of Galilee, Andrews. He was murdered by Arabs. 5. Rescuing a wounded man during 1937 disturbances. 6. A woman-guard at one of the "stockade and watchtower" settlements. 7. The Rothschild-Hadassah University Hospital, Mt. Scopus, Jerusalem. 8. Moshav Bet Yosef—a "stockade and watchtower" settlement in Beth She'an valley.

1. Arab terrorist bands on the march. 2. The trial of Shelomo Ben-Yosef, who was sentenced to be hanged. 3. Sir Harold MacMichael, Fifth High Commissioner. 4. Members of Jewish Settlement Police disarming an Arab marauder. 5. Martial law in Jerusalem. 6. Kibbutz Ma'aleh ha-Hamisha founded as "stockade and watchtower" settlement. 7. A defensive street blockade in the Jewish Quarter, Jerusalem. 8. Orde Wingate, commander of the Special Night Squads, and Moshe Shertok (Sharett). 9. Yizhak Sadeh at center with Moshe Dayan (left) and Yigal Allon (right) at the founding of Kibbutz Ḥanitah.

1939

1. Demonstration against the White Paper, Jerusalem. 2. Kibbutz Bet ha-Aravah, near the Dead Sea. 3. The illegal immigrants of the "Parita" disembark on Tel Aviv beach. 4. Operation at the Hadassah University hospital on Mt. Scopus. 5. German immigrants at Herzliyyah. 6. Group of settlers tents near Gederah. 7. The Jewish delegation to the St. James Conference in London.

2

3

4

5

1. Procession of recruits to the British Army, Tel Aviv. 2. The office of "Davar" newspaper after British search, Tel Aviv. 3. Diamond polishing factory in Netanyah. 4. Tel Aviv after air-attack by Italians. 5. The deportation ship "Patria" sinking in Haifa bay after Haganah sabotage.

1941

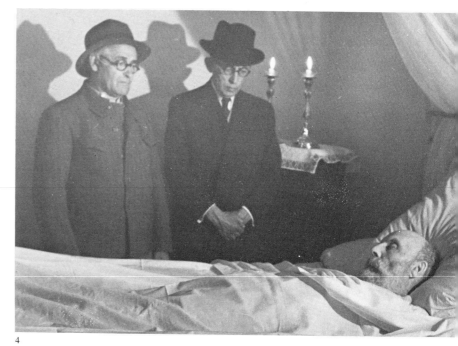

1. The Mufti in Germany. 2. Some of the 23 Haganah volunteers who were lost at sea while on British commando mission. 3. Palmaḥ is organized. 4. Menahem Mendel Ussishkin on his death bed. Avraham Harzfeld and Moshe Novomeysky stand by. 5. Allenby street, Tel Aviv.

1. Dr. Chaim Weizmann addressing the Biltmore Conference, New York. 2. Avraham Stern (Ya'ir), founder of Loḥamei Ḥerut Israel. 3. The "German Squad" of the Palmaḥ on a training march. 4. Jewish Palestinian ATS women. 5. Sabbath service of a British Army Jewish unit in the Western desert.

1943

1. British arms-search at Kibbutz Ramat ha-Kovesh. 2. Warsaw Ghetto uprising. 3. The fortress-like synagogue of Neveh Ya'akov. 4. Kibbutz Revivim founded. 5. "Teheran Children"—refugees from Poland via Iran, arrive. 6. Yemenite immigrants arrive. 7. Women recruits to WAAF.

HEADQUARTERS
JEWISH BRIGADE

מטה
הבריגדה היהורית

No Motor Cycles
Past this Point.

IN

1. The funeral of Berl Katznelson, Tel Aviv. 2. Berl Katznelson. 3. Brigadier E. F. Benjamin, commander of the Jewish Brigade. 4. The first dance festival at Kibbutz Daliyyah. The Paratroopers. 5. Enzo Sereni. 6. Hannah Szenes. 7. Jewish Brigade Headquarters in Egypt.

1945

1. The funeral of Henrietta Szold. 2. Jewish Brigade soldiers guarding German prisoners of war. 3. Youth Aliyah brings new immigrants. 4. Palestinian papers declare V.E. Day. 5. Mother and daughter re-unite. 6. Tel Aviv welcomes home 500 Palestinian prisoners of war. 7. Concentration camps are liberated.

1. Ben-Gurion testifying before the Anglo-American Committee of Enquiry regarding the problems of European Jewry and Palestine. 2. Buber and Magnes before the committee. 3. Holocaust survivors on their way to Palestine. 4. The Jewish Agency's "Bureau for Missing Relatives". 5. Jewish Agency Executive members arrested on "Black Saturday"—L. to R. David Remez, Dov Joseph, Moshe Shertok (Sharett), David ha-Cohen. 6. "Illegal" immigrant resisting deportation to Cyprus. 7. Demonstration against British rule. Soldiers try to arrest a youth. 8. "Illegal" immigrant girl interrogated by British soldiers. 9. Chaim Weizmann lays the foundation stone for Weizmann Institute of Science in Reḥovot.

1947

1. Weizmann before United Nations Special Committee on Palestine. 2. Joy at UN decision to partition Palestine. 3. Kibbutz Haogen, newly founded. 4. Acre prison, scene of the IZL operation to liberate their comrades. 5. "Illegal" immigrants boarding life raft before embarkation on Haganah ship "Unafraid".

3

THE PALESTINE POST

JERUSALEM
SUNDAY, MAY 16, 1948

PRICE: 25 MILS
VOL. XXIII. No. 6714

THE PALESTINE POST

THE SUBSCRIPTION DEPARTMENT has returned to The Palestine Post offices, Hasolel Street, Jerusalem, Tel. 4235.

STATE OF ISRAEL IS BORN

The first independent Jewish State in 19 centuries was born in Tel Aviv as the British Mandate over Palestine | same time, President Truman announced that the United States would accord recognition to the new State. A few | iator but without taking any action on the Partition Resolution of November 29.

DF troops capture Beersheba from the Egyptians. 2. Housewives line up for water in the besieged city of Jerusalem. 3. Ben-Gurion reads the Israel Declaration of Independence in Tel v. 4. Headline of the Palestine Post, May 16, 1948. 5. First boatload of legal immigrants arrives two days after creation of State.

1949

1. A guard of honor at Lydda airport receives the remains of Theodor Herzl, brought for reburial in Jerusalem. 2. Jewish immigrants, held by the British in detention camps in Cyprus. 3. [.] Weizmann at the opening of the Weizmann Institute. 4. Israel becomes a member of the UN. 5. Reburial of the war's dead soldiers. 6. Enthusiastic Tel Aviv crowds obstruct the first Independence Day Parade.

Beduin tribesmen in Beersheba participate in the Independence Day celebrations. 2. Jerusalem is divided. 3. Immigrants learn Hebrew. 4. 170,000 immigrants arrive this year. 5. Lilienblum, e "black market" street in Tel Aviv. 6. 45,000 Yemenites arrive by "Magic Carpet" airlift. 7. Snow in Jerusalem.

1951

1. Polish immigrants. 2. Kurdish immigrants. 3. Iraqi immigrants. 4. *Ma'barah* (temporary camp) in Tiberias.

1

1952

3

5

7

President Iẓḥak Ben Zvi meets heads of local churches. 2. King Hussein of Jordan. 3. The President of Israel, Chaim Weizmann dies. 4. Israel and German representatives sign repatitions agreement. 5. The new Israel pound note is issued. 6. Unemployment grows. 7. Phosphate produced at Oron in the Negev.

1953

1. Immigrant son meets his father again in Israel. 2. Arab terrorists attack Moshav Tirat Yehudah. 3. A new road links Beersheba with the Dead Sea. 4. A terrorist mine derails a train near Haifa. 5. "Conquest of the Desert" exhibition in Jerusalem. 6. Ultra-Orthodox demonstration in Jerusalem.

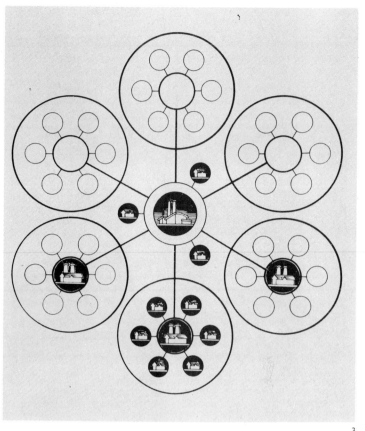

Arab terrorists ambush a bus to Elath. 2. Egyptians seize the Israel ship *Bat Galim* in the Suez Canal. 3. Lachish regional planning diagram. 4. Archeologists uncover Bet She'arim cata-
ombs. 5. Unexpected agricultural surplus causes dilemma. 6. Jordanians shell Jewish Jerusalem. 7. Moroccan immigrants in their new home in the Judean hills.

1955

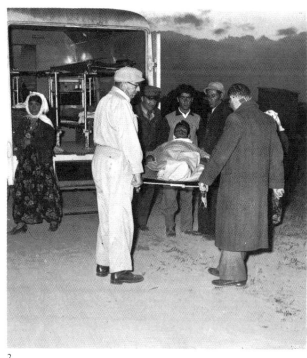

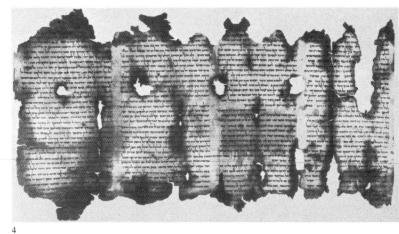

1. Army holds first four-day march. 2. *Fedayeen* attack wedding party at Moshav Patish. 3. Tel Aviv revives Purim *Adloyada*. 4. Israel acquires Dead Sea Scrolls. 5. Army introduces Uzi submachinegun. 6. Yarkon–Negev water pipeline. 7. Potash production at the Dead Sea. 8. Dimona, a new link to the Dead Sea.

1956

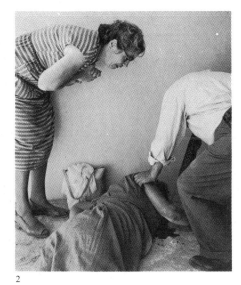

1

2

3

4

5

6

7

8

1. Terrorists kill woman in Ashkelon. 2. Jordanians kill four members of an archeological convention at Ramat Rahel. 3. Army retaliates at Qualqiliya. 4. At Sharm-el-Sheikh Egyptians block Israel ships from Red Sea. 5. Gamal Abdul Nasser. 6. British tanks patrol Port Said. 7. Dag Hammerskjöld. 8. Israel forces move against Egypt and occupy the Sinai Peninsula and the Gaza Strip.

1957

1. Eilat-Haifa oil pipeline completed. 2. The Haifa Technion builds a new campus on Mt. Carmel. 3. Kaiser-Frazer manufactures cars in Haifa. 4. Kafr Qasim *sulha* (meal of reconciliation). 5. Druze are recognized as independent religious community. 6. Mann Auditorium, Tel Aviv, home of the Israel Philharmonic Orchestra, inaugurated. 7. Israel withdraws from Sinai.

1

2

3

4

5

6

7

1. Spectators watch the parade. 2. First International Bible Quiz held in Jerusalem. 3. Independence Day Parade in Jerusalem. 4. Michael Bodrov, Soviet Ambassador, presents credentials. 5. Hebrew University opens new campus at Givat Ram. 6. Diesel trains replace steam locomotives. 7. Syrians shell Kibbutz Ḥulatah.

1959

1. Tel Aviv celebrates 50th anniversary. 2. Gershon Agron, mayor of Jerusalem, dies. 3. The Wadi Salib (Haifa) riots. 4. Tel Aviv Museum opens Helena Rubinstein Pavilion. 5. Queen Elisabeth of Belgium opens Hebrew University Archeology Institute. 6. Kiryat Yovel, a new district in Jerusalem. 7. Timna copper mines begin operation.

1. Bar Kokhba letters found in Judean Desert caves. 2. Ben-Gurion meets with De Gaulle in France. 3. Atomic reactor opened at Naḥal Sorek. 4. Hadassah opens new medical center.

1961

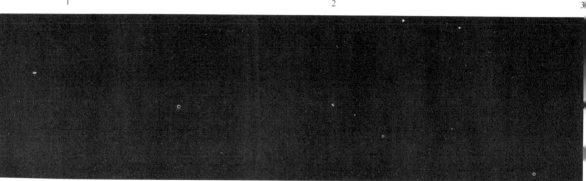

1, 2, 3. The first Israel Music Festival takes place in the Roman theater at Caesarea. Pablo Casals (left) and Isaac Stern (right) perform there. 4. Adolf Eichmann is brought to justice in Jerusalem. 5. The memorial for the six million at Yad Vashem, Jerusalem.

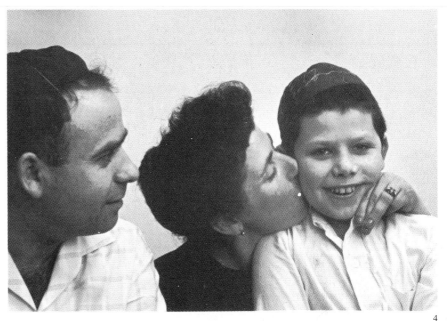

1. Ivory Coast President Houphouet-Boigny visits Israel. 2. President Ben-Zvi visits Africa. 3. Brother Daniel claims his right to an immigration certificate under the "Law of Return" and for registration as a Jew. 4. Yossele Schumacher, abducted by his grandfather and orthodox extremists, rejoins his family. 5. Tell el Milh, site of Canaanite Arad, excavated. 6. "Arad" in Hebrew inscription on potsherd. 7. Modern Arad.

1963

1. President Ben-Ẓvi dies. 2. Levi Eshkol becomes prime minister. 3. Zalman Shazar becomes third president. 4. Postal workers strike. 5. Hebrew Union College opens Jerusalem branch. 6. Military service shortened to 26 months. 7. First Reḥovot Conference for Developing Countries. 8. Yigael Yadin begins excavations at Masada.

Naḥal settlement at Modi'in. 2. Levi Eshkol meets Lyndon Johnson in the U.S. 3. World Chess Olympics in Tel Aviv. 4. Pope Paul VI visits the Holy Land. 5. Isaac Nissim elected Sephardi Chief Rabbi. 6. Town of Karmi'el established in Central Galilee. 7. Egyptian pilot defects to Israel.

1965

1. Teddy Kollek mayor of Jerusalem. 2. The Israel Museum opens in Jerusalem. 3. Rolf Pauls, first German ambassador to Israel. 4. Martin Buber dies. 5. Levi Eshkol meets President Jomo Kenyatta of Kenya during Africa visit. 6. Ambassador Ben Nathan (r.), with German President Luebke. 7. Eli Cohen, "Our Man in Damascus" is hanged. 8. Wolfgang Lotz ("Our Man in Cairo") and his wife. 9. Moshe Sharett dies. 10. First ship arrives at newly built Ashdod port.

Israeli troops destroy al-Fatah base at Samū. 2. Konrad Adenauer meets Naḥum Goldmann on visit to Israel. 3. The Knesset moves into its new Jerusalem building. 4. Israelis help up moshav-type village in the Ivory Coast. 5. Rostropovich plays with the Israel Philharmonic Orchestra. 6. Citrus exports exceed $75,000,000. 7. Shmuel Yosef Agnon receives Nobel ize for Literature.

1967

1. Israel armored columns advance across the Sinai Peninsula. 2. Egyptian military column at Mitla Pass is destroyed. 3. Troops arrive at the Suez Canal. 4. Soldiers arrive at the Western Wall. 5. The Navy moves to Sharm-el-Sheikh. 6. An improvised memorial on the spot where soldiers fell in Jerusalem.

3

5

7

ourists shop in the Old City. 2. View of the Western Wall. 3. Excavations begin at the southern end of the Temple Mount. 4. The World Jewish Economic Conference meets in Jeru- m. 5. Old people demonstrate in Jerusalem against the indifference of the authorities. 6. Israel television opens broadcasts. 7. Flower exports reach peak at the Christmas season.

1968

1969

1

2

3

4

5

6

7

1. Election posters. 2. East Jerusalem Arabs vote in municipal elections. 3. Herut meets to choose ministers for the National Coalition Government. 4. Immigrants from Latin America. 5. Luxury apartments under construction in Jerusalem. 6. Arab schoolboys near Jericho erect defenses against terrorist shelling from Jordan. 7. Navy missile boats brought from Cherbourg despite French embargo.

MM-6) AMMAN, Jordan, Sept.9 (AP) — Some hostage passengers and crew members of the hijacked TWA and Swissair jetliners squat in sand in front of their captive 'plane on Jordanian airstrip North of Amman, pt.8. (AP Radiophoto) (rjp 9/9/70 amm/str/rrr)

2

4

6

1. Arab terrorists hijack three planes and hold passengers in the Jordanian desert. 2. Children take shelter at Kibbutz Merom Golan during Syrian artillery attack. 3. Cease-fire at the Suez Canal. 4. Arab terrorists ambush school bus, killing twelve. 5. Arab terrorists bomb Moshav Elkosh in Upper Galilee. 6. Hanna Meron returns from Munich after injury from terrorist attack on El Al plane.

1971

1. Japanese pilgrims pray at the Western Wall for the peace of Jerusalem and for Soviet Jewry. 2. Israel's three millionth citizen (r.) arrives from Leningrad. 3. Four African presidents visit Israel in effort to make peace in the area. 4. Israel air force Stratocruiser shot down over Sinai by the Egyptians. 5. New Tel Aviv Museum building opened. 6. "Black Panthers" protest social and economic gap in Israel society. 7. Kibbutzim increase industrialization. 8. Meyer Lansky, U.S. underworld figure, expelled from Israel. 9. Affluence comes to the kibbutz.

1972

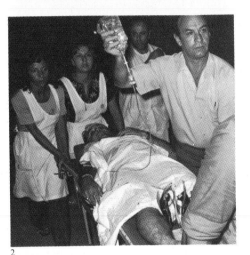

2

3

4

6

8

1. New pier at Gaza Port. 2. Lydda airport massacre. 3. Kozo Okamoto, Japanese terrorist, on trial. 4. Security search of air passengers before boarding planes at Lydda airport. 5. Residents of Arab countries arrive for summer visits. 6. Former residents of Beram demonstrate to return to their village. 7. Satellite communications station opened in Emek Ha-Elah. 8. "Black Panthers" continue to protest.

1973

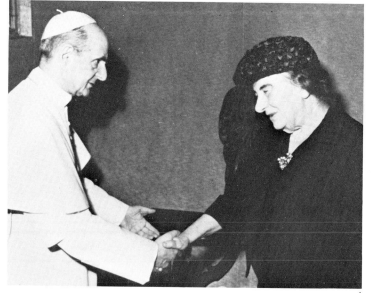

1

2

6

1. Israel PM Golda Meir meets Pope Paul VI at Vatican. 2. "Reshef" first Israeli-made missile boat. 3. Fly-past of fighter planes on Israel's 25th Independence Day. 4. Prof. Ephraim Katzir—Israel's fourth president. 5. Yom Kippur War—reporting for duty. 6. Israel's POW's return from Egypt. 7. The Golan Heights. 8. Cease-fire agreement signed between Egypt and Israel. 9. Agranat judicial inquiry commission appointed to investigate events connected with War.

1. West Bank of Suez Canal is evacuated. 2. Soldiers rescue children held hostage during terrorist attack on school at Ma'alot. 3. Protest demonstration in Jerusalem against Moshe Dayan. 4. A Beth Shean apartment after Arab terrorist attack. 5. President Nixon on official state visit in Israel. 6. PM and Mrs. Rabin welcomed in the White House by President and Mrs. Ford. 7. Israel POW's return from Syria. 8. Black Panthers demonstrate against new economic policy. 9. Gala performance of Valery and Galina Panov in Israel.

1975

1. The Israel-made "Kfir" fighter plane. 2. Savoy Hotel, Tel Aviv, after terrorist attack. 3. Eliyahu Bet Zuri and Eliyahu Hakim, who killed Lord Moyne in Cairo in 1944, brought burial in Israel. 4. Rabin at Bergen-Belsen memorial for Holocaust victims. 5. Kissinger arrives in Israel for Israel-Egypt disengagement agreement. 6–7. Anti- and pro-interim agreeme rallies. 8. Oil workers autographing the flag before handing over Abu Rudeis. 9. Rabin and Kissinger meet in Germany. 10. "I am a Zionist" rally, protesting UN anti-Zionist decisio

3

4

5

6

7

8

9

David Elazar, former chief-of-staff, buried. 2. Hadassah hospital on Mt. Scopus re-opened. 3. Jonathan Netanyahu, commander of the Entebbe rescue operation, was killed during the
d. 4. A Hercules plane which took part in the mission. 5. IDF soldiers arrive to the rescue. 6. The rescued hostages arrive in Israel after release. 7. Americans of White Russian origin
rive on first charter plane from US West Coast. 8. Israeli medical tent at "Good Fence" for aiding Lebanese citizens. 9. Miss Israel, Rina Mor, is crowned Miss Universe.

1977

1

2

3

4

5

6

1. Israeli and Lebanese boys before football match in Nahariya. 2. Rabin voted head of Labor Movement. 3. Maccabi Tel Aviv basketball team wins European Championship. 4. The Maccabi team at welcome home reception. 5. Pre-election posters in Jerusalem. 6. PM Begin meets US President Carter in Washington. 7. The historic meeting between Egypt's President Sadat and Israel's PM Begin in Jerusalem. 8. Begin replying to Sadat's speech at the Knesset. 9. President Sadat prays at Al-Aqsā Mosque. 10. Mena House Hotel, near Cairo.

. Protest rally against Israel's possible ceding of Yamit area. 2. Ezer Weizman, Israel Minister of Defense, in Cairo. 3. Israel-Egypt military conference, Cairo. 4. Chip Carter, President Carter's son, visits Western Wall. 5. Ezer Weizman and Egypt's Minister of War, Gamasy, in Cairo. 6. International Jewish Cooking Competition, Jerusalem. 7. Political round-table talks at the Jerusalem Hilton. 8. Shiloh—a new settlement in Samaria. 9. Raphael Eytan, appointed eleventh Chief of Staff. 10. Israeli oranges poisoned in Europe with mercury.